*The Joy Addict*

books by James Harms

*Modern Ocean*
*The Joy Addict*

Tony,

# The Joy Addict

Welcome to
West Virginia!
We're lucky
you're here

poems by

*James Harms*

In friendship,
J

Carnegie Mellon University Press
Pittsburgh 1998

## Acknowledgments

Grateful acknowledgment is made to the editors of the following magazines in which some of these poems were first published, occasionally in different form:

*American Voice* (*"Fin de Siecle,"* "The Tables on the Patio"); *Another Chicago Magazine* ("Autobiography as Slide Show"); *Antioch Review* ("Epithalamium," "Sky"); *Chicago Review* ("Reel around the Shadow"); *College English* ("Cheever" as "The Other World"); *Denver Quarterly* ("Tomorrow, We'll Dance in America"); *The Gettysburg Review* ("After Yes," "The Friend Who Never Married"); *Hayden's Ferry Review* ("Theoretical Life"); *Illinois Review* ("Los Angeles"); *The Journal* ("As Always"); *Kestrel* ("East of Avalon"); *The Missouri Review* ("Decadence: Newport Beach, California," "20th Century Boy"); *New England Review* ("Mariner Without a Moon," "Wherever You Hang Your Head"); *Passages North* ("At the Rally to Protest," "If All of Us Worry"); *Poet Lore* ("Sick of Food"); *Poetry* ("From Ocean Park to Healdsburg," "Mrs. Worthington"); *Poetry East* ("The Joy Addict"); *Poetry Northwest* ("Field Trip to My First Time"); *Southern Poetry Review* ("Close Your Eyes and Go to Heaven"); *Thin Air* ("Now that Stephen's Back"); *Quarterly West* ("My Own Little Piece of Hollywood"). An earlier version of "Tomorrow, We'll Dance in America" was reprinted in *Pushcart Prize XVIII: Best of the Small Presses 1993-1994*. The following poems appeared in *East of Avalon*, a letterpress edition from Caddis Case Press, illustrated and designed by Margaret Sunday: "Decadence: Newport Beach, California," "Close Your Eyes and Go to Heaven," "Wherever You Hang Your Head," "Field Trip to My First Time," "East of Avalon," "Theoretical Life," and *"Fin de Siecle."*

The author would like to thank the PEN American Center and the Revson Foundation for a fellowship that was of tremendous help in the completion of this book. Thanks also to the Pennsylvania Council on the Arts for a fellowship in creative writing, West Virginia University for a Senate Research Grant, and the Radiological Consultants Association for a Summer Fellowship. The author is indebted to the following for the cover of this book: Julie Scott, who painted the image; Linda Warren for the design; Westcott Press for the printing; Jeff Carpenter, good and true friend, for making it all happen. And finally, the author thanks these friends for their comments and advice: Ralph Angel, Peter Cameron, David Wojahn and Dean Young.

The publication of this book is supported by a grant from the Pennsylvania Council on the Arts.

Library of Congress Catalog Card Number 97-65557
ISBN 0-88748-265-1
ISBN 0-88748-281-3 Pbk.
Copyright ©1998 by James Harms
Printed and bound in the United States of America

10  9  8  7  6  5  4  3  2  1

# Contents

## *four*

*for Paige*

*How sad to love everything*
*And not to know what we love!*

—Juan Ramon Jimenez

*one*

# Sky

Last night a few years ago my sister
waited by the phone with a wooden spoon
and when it finally rang she beat it
and began to cry. Neither I nor
my mother made attempts to get near
that phone. Our house those years
was a block away from Christmas Tree Lane,
a row of deodars that ran without break
from Woodbury Street to Altadena Drive.
Indigenous to Nepal, the deodar is fine
in the thin air of the Himalayas, less adept
at discerning $CO_2$ from the solitary
molecule of smog. So now there are
gaps in the lane where the dying
trees have been cut up and dragged away.
The lights at Christmas are more obvious
and somehow garish, shocking, hanging free
where once were branches. When I was twenty
I considered lying down in front
of the crane used to remove my parents'
enormous eucalyptus. It robbed the garden
of water, they said, it would kill them
one day, drop a limb through the roof.
Instead of protest, I took a lawn chair
and a six-pack on the patio and watched the men
work their way down from the delicate
top branches, chopping for hours, finally
sawing off the trunk at the ground.
In a few years my sister's baby
will be old enough to listen attentively.
I'll walk with her through the backyard
beyond the terrace, her hand up high
in mine like a child at the fair attached
to a balloon. We'll step onto the stump,
flush now to the earth and ringed

with St. Augustine. There will be room
enough to dance with one so small.
And when she asks how tall it was,
the bluegum eucalyptus that held and hid
the stars I looked for from my
bedroom window, and caught the few that fell,
it will be easy enough just to point
to a particular spot in the sky.

# Field Trip to My First Time

No one called from the foot of the stairs.
But there we were anyway, showered
and snug in a fresh pair of jeans,

the table arrayed with toast
and two flavors of jelly;
it was difficult leaving the house.

The bus driver waited at the corner, engine idling
like a kitten in his lap, and everyone smiled
as we boarded. . . .

And in the end
we couldn't have known:
the brown grass for miles, like a sea

grown tired of rising into the sky,
of falling in pieces
so far from home,

the live oaks and lupine,
the dust, the picnic benches
crowded into the shade,

the other children and their same brown sacks,
three kinds of soda in a chest
by the bus.

And then the walk to the falls,
the three forbidden pools, a man
in a round hat, his skin as brown

as a belt, yelling above
the roar, explaining the story of snow
and spring, the long fall

to the bay, which we could "see in the distance,"
though none of us could, the smog
as thick as a filthy sweater.

Then Helen asked about Manuel,
whose sweatshirt hung from a yucca tree
at the foot of Falls Trail.

Someone yelled, "Search party!"
but Mrs. Ingalls insisted we sit.
And the man like a belt

left his hat with Bill Norton,
who wouldn't wear it, just balanced it
on his knees like a plate of hot food.

We tried to sing "Michael Row Your Boat"
but Mrs. Ingalls hissed.
"What about Twenty Questions?" suggested Sally Lee.

And so we waited without worry for the man
to return with Manuel, who fell
without a sound

from just below the top,
mixed in with the swirling water
and slid from one pool to the next,

then floated by us like a clump of old sticks;
we almost didn't notice him. I'd never seen
someone dead. It was my first time.

# Decadence: Newport Beach, California

Sure it's bright, a good day by some standards.
A child staggers past on plastic skates
still stepping instead of rolling,
oblivious to her own blonde hair

exploding in the wind,
to the crowd of joggers piling up
behind her, who run in place
and check their watches as if

her balance is their custody,
a crystal vase they must carry
for the time it takes her
to work out this new knowledge.

Another kid plays with a sail on the beach,
gets tangled up in canvas
on the slim strip of sand.
He looks like a tiny mummy, but no one's watching

so no one's scared, except him:
he fears the tide's soft fingers,
the Christmas lights floating in the sticky water, a plastic
wine glass, a strand of kelp. And it's hard to breathe.

Such a long list of fears, really,
for one so young.
And Larry the can man can't stand it,
Larry the can man

who owns this particular route, who is
screaming about the noise the sun is making
and he's got a point: it's hard to hear the light
dancing on the water with all this glare.

So when the century ends instead of the world
and we sip our last beers on the pier,
the strange gold light
like dust on the water. . . .

And there she goes, a woman tan beyond beauty,
somewhat drunk and smiling;
she walks off the dock as if feigning disgrace.
In all the confusion

her infant son crawls away
and finds the abandoned sail, lifts it up, disappears.
While around us the houses huddle
in the wind, which tears the sun

from the little skater's hair
and rips the harbor into pieces,
chips of light between the boats
like bottle glass on broken pavement.

Larry wails for broken bottles
but he's seeing things,
he's looking right at us. No.
It's the ocean over our shoulders; he's looking at that.

## 20th Century Boy

It's true, the cure has come through, though we can't
afford it: sometimes the music mistakes us
for instruments, sometimes not. And the girl
from another planet, who once said, "You've got me
in your pocket," she isn't really here, though the silence
that surrounds her is enough to drop us through
sidewalks and subway grates, to the cracked river curving
away into darkness. They say a lamplit face is perfect
until we try to explain what we've seen. But the truth is,
it's easier to look without seeing than say anything at all.

## Sick of Food

*after Mark Eitzel*

You gave me my favorite shirt.
It's sort of green
and almost yellow, and I've been up
and in it since dawn,
sitting on the stairs
of your building with the seagulls;

they're waiting for me
to pull my hand out of a bag of doughnuts.
I want to know what I did last night
and a few other things,
but mostly if I said
to you what I remember saying

or if it was a dream.
We could eat first, then talk about it
or vice versa, but I forget
whether you come home
at ten or at twelve,
and I'm hungry.

I wish you were here to talk to.
But if you were we probably wouldn't,
or I'd say, Forget it,
and you'd say, Never mind.
In the meantime
I'm afraid

the gulls will take my hand off
if I pull it out of the bag.
I'm afraid of other things, too,
so I just don't move.
I watch the street fill up with fog,
these narrow blocks near the Castro,

until I'm wrapped in it
and shivering.
You'll be home soon.
I'll play you my new tape
of rain falling in a forest;
it's kind of cheesy, but nice.

I bought you the book that goes with it,
pictures of trees dripping, and shiny frogs.
Facing each other in your window seat,
our legs braided
and the stereo murmuring like water,
we'll feel like we're inside something together,

the fog closing down the day
and you and I leaning a little
toward each other, as if we were born
with just one kiss and this is it: now what?
It's almost eleven.
I guess you get home at noon.

Across the street has disappeared;
I'm whistling on your stairs
to keep the fog out of my mouth.
I hope when you get here
you'll let me stay.
I'll say I'm sorry for what I said,

even if it's true.
And with one kiss left
we'll walk out in the fog
holding hands. We both know
what it's like to be with someone we can't see,
going somewhere that isn't, necessarily, there.

## If All of Us Worry

If I end this way on this street,
with this mistaken idea of myself,
a bunch of "unspent potential,"
my friends will drop their hands
in their laps and nod,
like couples gathered for dinner
discussing salad dressings
and the movies.

"I'm still alive," says a man wrapped
in oil cloth shaking his can, as the rest of us
pinch ourselves and drop our lunch bags
in the trash. Lovers share
a sandwich and a bench and speak
with their mouths full. Pigeons surround
the elderly and make demands.
I stop to buy an ice cream
from a truck at Washington Square
and join a line of strangers and their briefcases,
each with a recent haircut,
all of us growing younger as we
move forward. In front of me
a woman wears wonderfully a pretty dress,
lime owls on a periwinkle background,
and she orders chocolate, then changes her mind.
"Make that pistachio please . . . I'll have pistachio."
She turns to me and pulls
her purse strap higher on her shoulder.
"I'm going to have pistachio," she says,
and she holds her dollar bill
as if she found it on the sidewalk.
"Good idea," I say,
and look up at the happy vendor.
"I'll also have pistachio."
"Two pistachios," he says, "coming right up."

Around us the avenue
is falling to its knees, as if everywhere
on the ground are dollars to be collected,
autumn leaves in early June,
aberrant and green. Years go by
in lines. Years go by in arguments.
Years go by in love, and then, sometimes, alone.

"Could you make that a double?" I ask,
and the vendor winks.
"You must love pistachio," the woman says.
"Oh I do, I do."
I look at the statue of Garibaldi
drawing his sword and say,
"I've always loved pistachio,
I just never knew it until now."

# From Now On

When Ron and Lisa split up, she took a job
at her brother's bar, while he went
upstate to a place like Frank Martin's
in "Where I'm Calling From,"
to "gain a few pounds," he said,
though what he meant was that he'd lost
everything and wanted some of it back.

I don't think I've lost as much,
though some mornings I sit with coffee
at a window facing the harbor
and watch the tide fall beneath the boats all day;
it puts me closer to the friends I don't see anymore.
Toby used to drive from San Clemente
to Malibu on an average Saturday

looking for waves, and I'm almost certain
he's alive somewhere. And Tod I bet
is sailing, always sailing. I guess hope
is a swallow building its nest near the window,
winter on the wind, the storms shifting from
south to north, every omen saying *leave* . . .
but here comes the waitress with more coffee.

Ron came back and Lisa simply opened the door
and shut it behind him, no big deal, a few shrugs.
Her brother gave him work, and now Ron
is another alcoholic bartender, which is how
I met him. We can see the waves from
his window as he sets out the drinks
for the regulars, who leave before three

and return after ten, when the tourists
have taken their sandy bathing suits
and burned skin home to the wide valleys

filled with smog. Ron pours us each
a cup of decaf, which we sip
as we watch the parking lot empty, the beach
beyond empty, as we watch the surfers

paddle out for the next big set.
Ron and I retired our longboards a few years ago.
What we like now is the burnished look of a wave
at sunset, how the water streaks with black
as the crest trembles and pitches forward,
the ocean at the horizon a spill of Rose's
grenadine, a bottle of which sits behind Ron

on the shelf. Every once in a while he fixes us
Shirley Temples, sticks the little umbrellas in,
and we toast another day done well.
It's not that I've lost all that much.
Or that I want back what I've given away.
I just "need to get used to the changes,"
is what Ron says. He should know.

## Close Your Eyes and Go to Heaven

Someone's child took my hand
by mistake
in the supermarket checkout line. I bought her gum
from a machine. Outside

we fed the tin can nickels, watched
a slow-eyed Santa nod and ring a bell.
The child touched the bell, touched her lips,
touched the bell again. I kissed

the wooden horse and dropped a quarter
in the box, left her riding the endless road.
There are always two of us.

Someone dies with his beard above the covers.
I pull the blanket off and
close his eyes. A friend

puts his hand in my pocket and borrows cigarettes.
We talk to the same
pale woman at the party of
frantic gestures,
but we talk differently. She says, "How strange."

The party always ends early,
at the door to the kitchen, where everyone

smokes and watches
the food cook. It's late in life
for small talk, and we're all

just a little tired, which is why we smoke
and listen to the food cook. Her hand

ends its gesture and falls asleep beside my own.
If I touch her

we will have to begin again.
Somehow it isn't sad. It isn't sad
recounting
the one

good fist fight, the boy's lip
cracked and bleeding. "It's about time you said
you're sorry for that," she says.
"Not yet," I answer, staring at smoke. "Not yet."

*two*

---

# The Tables on the Plaza

Sometimes, almost always
after sunset, in the plaza's
deepest corners, where evening
is a wet shadow and a sailor
sharpens a stick against the wall,
where the insects rehearse
their one note and where, even now,
there is laughter being filled with a fist—
sometimes I recognize a face.

And always I am broken off,
swallowing a sip of beer.
As I fold in half a different face and slide it in my shoe.
With other photographs and money.
With a letter of introduction.
We are all trying to get somewhere.
Sometimes I see a face.

And sometimes I dream of this, this room
and its windows of smeared dust.
And how, on my way up the stairs,
cold hands hold mine in a hallway,
where old men sleep in piles like coats,
and the one word in each mouth is, *Please.*

You can come to such a room with plans for getting by,
plans for each hour of each day,
each day a day longer than you'd planned.

And as the street sweeper hoses down the plaza,
forcing wine and a pair of shoes toward
the drain beside the fountain, you can watch the wings
of ash-colored pigeons stretch in the mist
and drip their black water hard
on the stones. And you can wish
for whatever you want

as the waiters in stained aprons
slide the tables out from under awnings,
where all day you sat weighing
the coffee in your cup.
You can wish for the chair nearest
the plaza, or a slice of cheese
with your bread.

Or for the kiss
of a young girl
who complained of fever
as she kissed and burned your tongue
and neck and ears
and finally, shivering, slept
as you watched from the window her father,
a tailor in the shop beneath the palmist,
circle the square saying her name, saying, *Please.*

How softly she lifted your hand to her face,
the palmist, as if pulling a plate wet
from the steaming sink, as if to read your bruises
and smell the skin of every face you've held.

Ever since you wanted anything
you wanted this.
To know a town by the people who visit
the shadows near the plaza,
who will sit with you for coffee
and list their small sadnesses
before preceding you up the stairs
to a room whose one hanging light
is shadeless and blinds the windows,
and shoves the town away, to its knees beside the river.

And if you were me, you would laugh
quietly into your hands beside that river

for all behind you who no longer bother
to explain, as they walk out the door, where
they are going. They are going
to the tables on the plaza. They are going
to meet me.

## Reel around the Shadow

On South Street, above a burning trashcan, a rasta
roasts a pigeon on a stick.

The East River moves like a whisper
past voices held in hands, the shanty towns packed

with vagrants on the lam who sing around fires as if trying to
     forget
their previous lives, their different hymns mingling

into moans, like widows bathing in the river
or the moon dissolving, a candle flame sputtering in its wax.

"I came here to start a band," says a man on the corner,
a Johnny Cash-type gone to seed,

his guitar case open, no instrument in sight;
he tells stories instead of singing:

"I came here to broker fortunes but left mine in my other
     pants.
I came here instead of marrying her, so she named him after
     my brother.

I came here to paint in oils but I can't afford the canvas.
It's all requests," he says. "You pick the story."

When I wander my own way, as I do now,
without lifting a heavy coin from my pocket,

it's to leave the aura of one life
for the shadow surrounding another.

Two streets down, a few over, the sudden shower
from above, an insomniac hosing his pansies on a fire
     escape—

it's all feathers instead of lead, the weight
of moving through America from toll to toll as if

at anytime the signs will lead us to a normal life.
While under the arch at the end or beginning

of 5th Avenue, my ghost waits
with a sack of clementines for me to finish my rounds.

It's time, he says, kissing me on each cheek,
while gypsies rustle in the trees. The statues dismount

and lead their horses toward the fountain.
And everywhere in buildings, the elevators

rise toward roofs, where angels are landing,
the world prepared at last.

## Theoretical Life

It could be you wishing to say it clearly.
Waiting by the boat for the rain to stop.
The wood slick and soft: old wood, old boat.
But it isn't you. Throat filling with water,
it isn't you. And you're not here to help the stranded,
even with shoes, a second-hand coat. With whatever
we've shared: the weary winter moonlight, the silver buttons
such light leaves behind, scattered beneath the bed.
We keep our arms around each other when we can,
struck and stranded. When we can, we never let go.

## At the Rally to Protest

I should ask, later, on the patio, what you meant
by being alone across a room,
through politics
and the wonder of coats, rubber shoes, as outside
it snowed on the bonfire,
as the speaker explained how the war proceeds

and the rest of who we knew, some singly
and some together, ate french fries
with ketchup. I was sad, like a small boy.
You're a finch on a wooden swing. I have never
been so far north.

Your sleeves hung from the chair as the crowd
applauded. What will we do, I wondered,
to keep this feeling going . . .
we'll do anything.
I think I would rather
just kiss.

Outside a boy is draft age, sad, and he sits.

A page of newsprint blows
across the street.
Someone whispers at the next table
an insult to the speaker
or a glass of milk.
Each breath feels
slightly used.

When my aunt played piano,
with a candlemaker's soft hands,
I wished I knew you. But that was . . . when?

Years ago, before I knew you. And now here you are.
Tell me, if you are able, how it goes
where you sit across the room,
watching half-indifferently or with love
and too long, me.

# Mrs. Worthington

I watch my neighbor walk to the end
of his dock, lean out above
the water as if to see
the sunset beyond the harbor entrance.

This far back in the bay
dusk arrives like the gust of breath
preceding a rumor, evening
applying its make-up to the day.

We're both imagining the sun
smearing along the horizon, the ocean
dissolving another yellow pill,
halcyon or valium,

and we're thinking of her.
His dock is just long enough
to not quite see around their boat,
though he's heard her laugh, heard

the hiss and clank of crossing silverware.
They've set a card table on the boards
above the water; there's music playing;
it isn't Bach. If only their

candles would stay lit, if only the dock
were a little longer, he could see
if the laughter is real, if her eyes
hold the flame or swallow it.

She isn't happy. She told him once
while slipping on her sandals.
She told me, too, then kissed me.
I watch him watch for both of us.

## After Yes

There's nothing over there
behind the sacks of old newspaper.
There's nothing in the cigarette box.

In the glass bowl, no apples.
No peaches or late bananas.
In the well outside, water

but no bucket. No phone calls
flashing on the answering machine,
no hang-ups or warnings, no tired message

that ends, "Oh, hell, just call."
Outside, a breeze: no clouds, no moon.
No dew on the rye, no frost,

no shadow in the pocket of night.
No ghost behind the river oak, whispering,
"No sense worrying about it."

And in between dreams, she kicks
the blankets off, rolls toward
the open window, and there is

no one between her and the edge
of the bed, no soft collision
to save her from falling.

# Los Angeles

*The days change at night.*
—X

I drove today along the foothills
looking for relief in distances.
I found the distances.

~

In late spring in Los Angeles—
in the air beneath a streetlight,
above a swimming pool, a breeze
sweetened by jasmine and orange blossoms—
there is nothing to know
except the stillness that follows loss,
the quiet in the blood.

~

Sunlight in the canyons.
The rustle of doves
in the palm trees, squirrels in the ivy.
Half of what I hear or see
is memory; the other half is what
I'm now ignoring and eventually will dream.
And like the last lingering smoke
that curls away toward the desert,
it's easy enough to choke
on what's left of my city.

~

I drove today as if to somewhere.
I spun the dial left to find a song.
And the space between stations
was a thousand throats clearing,

the sound a phone makes
when you've answered out of habit
or hope and no one's there,
it hasn't even rung.

~

In Los Angeles in late spring,
what's unknowable is always an angel,
always quiet. And in my latest dream
of leaving, I couldn't hear her
when she spoke, couldn't
hug her for the wings.

*three*

# Autobiography as Slide Show

Now here's the part of me who wasn't wrong
after all, and he's happy, he's saying hello.
And there's Paul in New Orleans. I remember
Paul remembering where the first crack
appeared in his marriage, then saying how
she never liked any of his friends,
which meant, I suppose, that she didn't like me,
then smearing another drop of hot sauce on an oyster.
There's nothing remarkable

to how we mend botched lives
by pressing lips to flesh and lying through the gash—
it's like ignoring the exit wound
and waking from the dream of being shot
knowing you'll sleep again. But I guess
that's the risk of doing anything at all,
talking through gulps of beer, ordering another tray
of oysters— the body can only take
so much plunder and unchewed food,

what it needs is to quit taking the blame.
When Paul made it work, healed his marriage
without my help and looked around quickly
as if ashamed, as if he'd heard his name called
and turned to see a scrap of tissue
and an empty bag blowing down the street, the months
of suffering a cunning fiction,
I couldn't believe it.
And I can't forget what he said about

what she said about me, which I see now
was his way of making me love him,
so uncertain he was that anyone could.

Either he's forgotten all that or it
wasn't true, which is a lie either way,
though the beer that night was cold
and we ordered more oysters than any two men
could eat. We ate them all.
Now here's the part of me in a red shirt

who believes someone could change his mind
like a pair of socks
or walk away without any at all, bony ankles
poking out beneath his blue jeans.
And no one's wrong anymore or maybe
everyone is but who cares?
Paul's happy or he thinks he is, and I'm not
sure if there's a difference.
And here I am waving at you. Do you remember?

# My Own Little Piece of Hollywood

*Maybe it's always Saturday in heaven.*
—The Jazz Butcher

I hate that particular dream
where she walks out of the hardware store
holding a rake and a sack of rye seed
and attempts to hug me—
I wake up scratching myself.
Worse yet is remembering
that she doesn't live here anymore,
not that she ever did with regularity.
But when we used to run into each other
now and then, there was a peculiar sort of
futility to our conversations that I miss;
I think it's because they so often
led to wistfulness, which is a derivation
of loneliness that I find companionable.
And in the other dream I hate
I'm back in the Roxy on Sunset Boulevard
watching the Replacements mangle
their last few songs, closing with
the theme from Gilligan's Island.
Bob Stinson's on guitar—
he throws up behind a speaker
without missing a note
while I pocket an ashtray and turn
to see a woman I used to go out with
pour her drink in her purse and walk away
without her wallet. And I'm trying
to move toward her table
to retrieve the wallet or yell or
something but there are all these people
between us and my voice sounds like
the wind behind a flock of
pigeons lifting off the pavement.

Then the band decides to keep playing.
I hear Paul Westerberg
start my favorite song in the middle
so he's singing,
"I'm so, I'm so, I'm so . . ."
and now he's screaming it,
the rest of the band gone on
with the song as it's written
but Paul stuck on that line,
screaming it over and over
like some pre-Altamont mantra,
until I know it's me singing
and I wake up sweating.
Sometimes there's someone
with me, someone looking at me,
and usually she's afraid.

# Now that Stephen's Back

*I love my drug buddy.*
—Evan Dando

Now that Stephen's back on drugs, he phones
at funny hours so we can
"talk without an audience," though we never talk;

Stephen likes to sing to me across the wires.
He thinks we live crowded lives, though I
live with Cathy and he's alone.

"The walls have ears," he says,
so we go out walking, skim our hands
atop the hedges, do-si-do the corner lamp post.

We cross the street to buy a magazine,
watch the vet invent a dance. We pay him
and cross back, wave at mannequins, tap the glass.

There's a grocery store
with lots of flowers, and Stephen tries
to name them all. He stops after "blue daisy."

At the ORBIT we shoot some pool, split a pitcher,
use the phone: Stephen pulls it in the bathroom
so he can "talk without an audience";

I listen from the hallway, but he flushes
whenever culpable. A pair of slackers
takes our game. They leave the eight ball

in a glass. When Stephen's done he comes out
smiling. We drink our beer, I say, So long.
Now that Stephen's back on drugs

he doesn't call to talk. "Are you there?" he says,
as if I'm not. I ease the door shut
so Cathy won't hear,

though she doesn't mind; she loves Stephen.
He says he'll prove he's getting better,
then he sings a song he wrote today.

It's pretty good, and I tell him so.
I say, Goodnight, Steve.
He says, OK.

## Tomorrow, We'll Dance in America

In America, there is an answer for everything,
though little has been asked.
We stand around the water cooler comparing notes.
If it is Friday, we discuss hope.

In America, in a bar, I sit beside . . .
well, her, for instance.
I expect the shadow boys in satin jackets
to emerge any moment from their rented corners,
distribute the bruised carnations.
Flowers are only a dollar, sometimes more.
It hurts to sit this close to someone
I will never know.

In America, I would be the first to say
someone has lied to us. Oh well.
Last year my lung turned black with empathy.
Please believe me when I say
all of this is a ruse for honesty.
In America, I can propose marriage to a pool of guppies.

In America I stand around wondering how to say
I love you, until she asks, Coffee?
I think I could live my whole life
waiting for someone to say the word
Love, knowing a cup of coffee was on its way.

# Fin de Siecle

Everyone is along for the ride,
though in the doorways in the cracks,
there are the few who have paused

and lifted empty wrists
to their ears, stopped for a smoke
in a slip of shade, wandered off

to watch the clouds refigure.
And the others, who in sight of everyone
lower their trousers for air,

or gather on benches to wait
for nightfall and a few friends,
the orchestra of invisible instruments:

John the bassoonist, Leroi the trombone,
Old Tom the slow tuba, sitting around
laughing, fingering the air,

a symphony of farts and belches.
Isn't this too real? Will anything
else do? A herd of zebras

on the yellow veldt? caught in slow mo
by a bored tourist?
And the little boy playing with

the venetian blinds, where are his parents
anyway? How could anyone so young
be left alone? And who is he signaling

so late in the century?

## The Friend Who Never Married

What if you lost the scrap of yellow paper
you've written your prayer on?

And in the corner of the mirror, your best friend's
son, his first school picture.

The new shoes are like the old ones.

~

You remember walking past your building one night,
the one lit window, the books piled on the table,
their spines facing out; you read the first three titles
before changing your mind about the person who lived there.

And the sound of snow falling on snow reminds you of
your friends trying to speak
through swallows of beer, the rows
of empty bottles, the twice-weekly drownings. . . .

~

The outgoing message: "I'm not home right now,
but if you leave your name. . . ."
The music in the background that gives you away.

~

Where is the cup of pens?
the ceramic frog? the dish of paper clips?

And the paperweight totems, the wax apple, the postcards
    tacked
to any empty space, where?

~

And what if the snow gathers
on your shoulders as you stand staring up
at a window waiting for your neighbor
to finish her shower?

The new shoes are like the old ones.
The prayer. The prayer.

## Wherever You Hang Your Head

I can see the stripes

of light across my father's face,
the blinds angled behind him, foothills
ragged through the slats

like a picture torn in strips
then reassembled. My sister
has her knees drawn up

beneath her on the chair and eats
a bowl of olives. Now
she is laughing into her napkin.

And look, my mother says,
pointing at the french doors.
A bird has stunned itself

against the glass, a sparrow,
its chest quaking, feathers bundled
on the patio. We all gather at the door.

It pulls itself together. It flies away
as if from us.

# Cheever

To study the world from a stoop, to fill
a pipe and ignore the violin
poking from a neighbor's trashcan,
the dog with three legs dressed
in a sweater.  Beyond the blue trees
the sky is gathering at the corners
like poorly folded laundry.
The husband dreams of starlings
who raise the curtain on morning,
and his wife slams the door.
It's good to have kept a few seeds
in a pocket, and now he places one
in the shadow of a leaf.
The new moon is a black beam in which
he leans forward on his knees
to spit on his thumbprint in the soil.
There's another world, he thinks,
right next to this one, over there.
Nearby a dog dreams of wolves,
a little boy of clear marbles,
there are black wings in blue branches.
The color gray is the color red
with less light.
Green turns to blue. Yellow to white.
So the other world is like the ocean
beyond the sun's painful touch,
where the reef blanches
and looks like concrete.
Where we grieve openly,
turn to see ourselves.
Where what we've made of our lives
drifts upward, weightless, toward the light.

# From Ocean Park to Healdsburg

Richard Diebenkorn, 1922-1993

Matisse left his fingerprints in the fire.
Beneath the cracked pitcher on a dresser.
On purple drapes, the light-splattered walls.
Mistakes were erased enough

to start again or continue,
but the finished shapes contain
their ghosts. And in the smudges,
in the faint, persisting pencil lines,

we see that he will die,
that nothing human is ever perfect,

even from the windows in Ocean Park.
Diebenkorn watched the landscape soften
and shift—he drew the miles, sketched
sky over sea;
what adds to distance more
than the color blue?

And in between he placed the power lines
and streets, bands of palm trees,
the torn sunlight in a corner.

But somewhere someone has rented a hall, hired a band,
is planning to drape the tables
with lavender linens.
The carpet is blue, a white runner
from door to stage; a daffodil
has dropped from her arms.
Fingers touch rice in a coat pocket,
the matchbook embossed with a date.

Now that the rains have come,
the yellow hills are raked with grass,
sage giving way to larkspur and poppy.
Beyond the forest is a mountain.
Beyond that, a field of dirt held back
for next year's onions.

Turning to his canvas, he pulls
it all into the studio, stretching
and stacking the empty valleys,
the wrinkled hills, the meeting halls
and eucalyptus.

And at the edges, blue.
As if to bridge these separate landscapes,
the vineyards of Healdsburg with Ocean Park,
today with hundreds of yesterdays.
Nothing perfect, but human.

And where the fit is poor
he scrapes and erases, paints again around
the ghosts, scrapes some more, turns to look.

*four*

## Mariner Without a Moon

The day I mistook the mailman
for Jesus, my wife brought home
a new friend. She introduced her
as someone who could help.
The friend and I went out to talk
in the shabby evening, sat
on the curb with our drinks.
Joe waved from up the street,
then threw a ball at his son,
who missed. Do you like it here?
she asked. What's it like to live here?
She kept swirling her glass
so I knew I had to say something.
It's okay, I said. It's peaceful.
I told her how in the mornings
sometimes people kneel
for their newspapers, cars
back up beside the hedges,
the dew sort of shines
if it's cold enough. Once,
I watched a little girl walk across
the wet grass in her socks
to kiss her Daddy goodbye.
The friend nodded her head
like I should keep going,
but I was finished.
When she left I swam alone
and sat for a while on the plastic
furniture in the moonlight.
Wrapped in a towel, I stared beyond
the pool to where my father
and a friend I'd been meaning to call
for fifteen years, someone
so buried in his hands

the silver light couldn't reach
his face, waited for me
to come walking.
I watched them circle the yard,
their shapes soft
in the pool's blue light.
Once, months ago, I tried to say hello
to them. Julia was shopping
for fabric, some silver pumps,
a few other things for her cousin's
wedding. We spent the morning
in a slow crawl through one
shop after another, had lunch
at the Crown City Cafe. It was
on Lake Street near the camera shop
that I turned to talk to one.
I guess this upset Julia.
She whispered my name three times
before she yelled it. And when I
turned I saw her face had a thin crack,
like a smile gone sour with misuse.
Since then I've ignored them.
I didn't tell the friend this.
We sat on the curb
in the rosy light and watched
Joe call in his kids.
I felt a hand on my shoulder.
She took a sip from her
glass of sun tea, but there
was only ice. I could hear it
crash against her teeth.
If you went with them, she said,
where do you think you'd go?
Someone's breath tickled my ear.
I pointed down the block,
toward where a boy I'd known once,
before he chased a butterfly
into a busy street, chalked
the sidewalk with squares.

Beyond him my father talked
to a man in a grey business suit.
She said, What's down there?
What do you see?
Nothing, I said, nothing.
I watched my father reach
for his wallet.
There's nothing there, I said.
But that's where I'd go.

## As Always

Now that we're okay, I guess we should finish
the dishes, straighten up, attend to things so long
neglected. Just look at the plants falling from
their pots, the cat so thin; I wonder where we've been.
Everything has grown a skin of dust (What is that song
you're whistling?), and the air tastes like lilacs.
But isn't it still December? We've been gone so long.

I'm not sure of this, but I remember holding
a hand that became a glass. And then the years—
those skeins of silk slipping from their folds,
the light trapped in places like blood fixed in a bruise.
It rained every day, umbrellas looming large
in the cramped doorways, the crowded vestibules; no one
knew they were passing inward to an airy dryness so severe
their clothes fell away like feathers. And for a while
we wore our organs outside our bodies.

But as always, there were those with expertise
and grace, who knew enough to help us back
into our clothes, back into the world.
I've never held a hand so long as his
who led me through alleys between buildings
to a shaft of daylight, a circle of warmth that shrank,
as I stood in it, to a spot on the sidewalk, a dime
I picked up and carried back to the world.

If we open the door and a window,
perhaps a breeze will lift away the dust,
though I feel light enough still to blow loose
of my body. Now that we're okay, there's very little
that keeps us here, which is why, perhaps, we stay.
I no longer hear the leaves as voices gathering
beneath the trees, in the gutters.
But I would recognize your heart if I saw it.

# East of Avalon

California, 1968

The slim boat rams the shore despite
the small boy's precautions.
He hauls the cargo hand
over glove up the narrow beach
toward home. But it wasn't home.
The parishioners loaned it to father
for the summer, though he stayed away
tending to the flock. And the nearby dock
held only the ferryman's shack and a few
rusted clamps. I dropped the pliers
in the water to watch them sink
and uncle forgave me.
When I quit trumpet to surf, my instrument
was made into several pairs of earrings
and a section of uncle's sculpture-in-progress.
It was only later that his madness
was mistaken for a reasonable vision
and he began his long, laborious retirement.
We wished him well each morning on our way
to the waves, his white painter's hat
dusted with flecks of ground brass.
And on borrowed surfboards or rented rafts
we rode, brother and I,
our flowered trunks flapping in the salty breeze,
the breakers crumbling at their edges
into soft shoulders. Sister opened
and shut her books, her tiny compact, a shoe
or bag of oranges at each corner
of the towel to anchor it down.
The cheers descended from the pier
like strips of Chinese fortunes as we rushed
toward shore and sister's flashing mirror.
And the carnival continued on the pier,
the big wheel turning like an ever-forming

thought in the sky's blue mind.
So many drove down from the foothills and valleys,
their white calves blazing above socks
and leather sandals, to stare
at the distant island, the parrots hooked
to dowels of wood and carried like flowers for sale
along the boardwalk, the tattoos crawling
across shoulders, down arms and into fists.
And everywhere the roar, the shift of sand
beneath the pilings, the plates of earth
squeezing past each other
like suitors at a dull, afternoon tea party,
the lady of the house upstairs having a nap.
The radio fit in my pocket like a wallet
and played the muffled hits as we
hopped barefoot across the boulevard,
salt glazing our backs like frost,
the peninsula a few blocks wide, the ferry ride
awaiting us: dolphins surfing
the bow wake, brother circling the boat
a few yards ahead of the fare collector,
who never looked up from counting change,
even when I gave him the extra quarter,
"honest to a fault," as uncle said.
Weekends mother appeared, weary from work
and the long drive, frightened of "such strong sun."
She waved from her huge hat, knees gathered
to her chest, waved from the tiny canvas chair
while we rehearsed our strokes in the quiet harbor:
Australian, side, breast and butterfly.
On buoys and anchored sail boats
the gulls turned to stone
and waited out the hazy mornings,
stretched their wings to dry.
Brother practiced picking off runners
at second base, casting shells across
the water at the fog-stunned birds:
every base was stolen, every runner safe.
Missives arrived from the north,

news about father and Robert Kennedy,
and someone mentioned the end of the season.
But for now the airy anteroom of summer
opened out onto boats at rest and islands,
a parade of families walking toward
the ice cream shop after dinner.
Avalon awaited a few miles across the channel,
visible when the winds blew inland the afternoon smog;
uncle promised to take us there
on the first dreary day, which was the day
we packed up the recently repainted '63 Impala
for the long ride home, where father
stood in the doorway with new gloves
for sister and the same sweatshirt
in different colors for brother and me.
Uncle spoke quietly beneath the deodar
to father, while mother backed the Chevy
down the driveway and waited behind the wheel,
car pointed toward the street.
Hours later, stacked in bunks
like seagoing gnomes, brother and I
fell to sleep slowly though certainly,
clay coins or contraband dumped
from a pirate's ship, the Queen's armada closing in—
fell toward our dreams, a distant bottom,
a dark continent of the blind. Outside
the engine idled beneath the trees
as uncle talked on and on and father listened,
the words rising into space,
each black syllable a curtain of meaning
extinguishing the stars as it passed,
so they seemed to wink off, then on.
And though we couldn't have known,
brother and I, so far
beneath the surface we'd fallen,
it was said later that father winked back
at the stars, that mother
saw the words drift away and pulled out
into traffic, that uncle found sister
sleeping on the patio, as if she, too,
had wished to watch the stars go out.

## The Joy Addict

Whales fall slowly to the ocean floor
after dying, and feed the vertical nation
for years. Like Christ, who feeds us still
they say, though I don't know.
But imagine it:
fish chasing through the bones
or nibbling what's left, the whale,
when it finally touches bottom,
an empty church.
Forget all that,
it's intended to soften
the skin, like apricot seeds and mud, or boredom.
The drift of worlds in a given day
can turn a telephone to porcelain,
open graves in the sidewalk. So that
who knows why thinking about thinking
leads to new inventions of grace
that never take, never lead to, say, what to do
with Grandmother, who is determined to live
"beyond her usefulness," which is fine,
but why won't she relax and watch the sea with me?
I wish someone would intrude on all this.
People grow tired
explaining themselves to mirrors,
to clerks administering the awful perfume.
I ask a Liberace look-alike,
"Why do you dress that way?"
"What way?" he says,
and he's right.
Who taught us to bow our heads
while waiting for trains? to touch
lumber without regret and sing privately
or not at all? to invest the season
with forgiveness and coax from it
a hopeful omen? Lord knows
the hope would heal this little fear.

But who taught us to fear?
Soon branches crackle in the windy heat
like something cooking too quickly,
dogwood lathering the empty woods
and everyone looking for a commitment
of permanence, from summer, from someone else.
Two deer the color of corn disappear
into an empty field, and I wait beside the road
for them to move. I want to see them again.

# Epithalamium

For once the clock radio ignites the day softly,
a slow song by Bessie Smith, and there's
a certain grace in the mingling of hair in a brush,
the easy long division of everything divided by two.

She takes a shower. He thumbs the window pane
to wipe away the steam, until it moans a little,
like wind through a picket fence; he watches the first
grade class walk by in a line, holding each others' sleeves.

Beginnings are a resource. And so he swipes
a pack of gum she's stowed in her coat pocket;
she borrows his sock to dust the furniture.
And in the quiet moment before they gladly take the blame

for familiarity and love, there's the knowledge
that it will all begin again soon: the soothing wake
of forgiveness and trust, a simple faith in the neverending,
how someone always rises from the chair, walks around the
       table,

lifts your chin like a nest blown from a branch,
kisses you. And then it starts all over again.

*Notes*

"Epithalamium" is for Bob and Amy Tafoya; "Theoretical Life" for Dean Young; "Sky" for Annemarie Mulry; *"Fin de Siecle"* for Aleda Shirley.

"From Now On" makes reference to Raymond Carver's short story "Where I'm Calling From" (*Cathedral*, NY: Knopf, 1983). The poem is loosely based on the song "To Her Door" by Paul Kelly, from his album *Under the Sun*. The poem "Now that Stephen's Back" is even more loosely based on the song "My Drug Buddy" by Evan Dando and The Lemonheads.

"Sick of Food" takes its title from the song of the same name by Mark Eitzel and the American Music Club; "20th Century Boy" from the song of the same name by Marc Bolan; "Los Angeles" from the song and album of the same name by X; "My Own Little Piece of Hollywood" from a line in the song "Girls Say Yes" by The Jazz Butcher (a.k.a. Pat Fish); "Mariner Without a Moon" from the short story "Rapture of the Deep" by Amy Hempel (*At the Gates of the Animal Kingdom,* NY: Knopf, 1990).

*Recent Titles in the Carnegie Mellon Poetry Series*

1990
*Why the River Disappears,* Marcia Southwick
*Staying Up For Love,* Leslie Adrienne Miller
*Dreamer,* Primus St. John

1991
*Permanent Change,* John Skoyles
*Clackamas,* Gary Gildner
*Tall Stranger,* Gillian Conoley
*The Gathering of My Name,* Cornelius Eady
*A Dog in the Lifeboat,* Joyce Peseroff
*Raised Underground,* Renate Wood
*Divorce: A Romance,* Paula Rankin

1992
*Modern Ocean,* James Harms
*The Astonished Hours,* Peter Cooley
*You Won't Remember This,* Michael Dennis Browne
*Twenty Colors,* Elizabeth Kirschner
*First A Long Hesitation,* Eve Shelnutt
*Bountiful,* Michael Waters
*Blue for the Plough,* Dara Wier
*All That Heat in a Cold Sky,* Elizabeth Libbey

1993
*Trumpeter,* Jeannine Savard
*Cuba,* Ricardo Pau-Llosa
*The Night World and the Word Night,* Franz Wright
*The Book of Complaints,* Richard Katrovas

1994

*If Winter Come: Collected Poems, 1967-1992,* Alvin Aubert
*Of Desire and Disorder,* Wayne Dodd
*Ungodliness,* Leslie Adrienne Miller
*Rain,* Henry Carlile
*Windows,* Jay Meek
*A Handful of Bees,* Dzvinia Orlowsky


1995

*Germany,* Caroline Finkelstein
*Housekeeping in a Dream,* Laura Kasischke
*About Distance,* Gregory Djanikian
*Wind of the White Dresses,* Mekeel McBride
*Above the Tree Line,* Kathy Mangan
*In the Country of Elegies,* T. Alan Broughton
*Scenes from the Light Years,* Anne C. Bromley
*Quartet,* Angela Ball


1996

*Back Roads,* Patricia Henley
*Dyer's Thistle,* Peter Balakian
*Beckon,* Gillian Conoley
*The Parable of Fire,* James Reiss
*Cold Pluto,* Mary Ruefle
*Orders of Affection,* Arthur Smith


1997

*Growing Darkness, Growing Light,* Jean Valentine
*Selected Poems, 1965-1995,* Michael Dennis Browne
*Your Rightful Childhood: New and Selected Poems,* Paula Rankin
*Headlands: New and Selected Poems,* Jay Meek
*Soul Train,* Allison Joseph
*The Autobiography of a Jukebox,* Cornelius Eady
*The Patience of the Cloud Photographer,* Elizabeth Holmes
*Madly in Love,* Aliki Barnstone
*An Octave Above Thunder: New and Selected Poems,* Carol Muske

1998

*Yesterday Had a Man in It,* Leslie Adrienne Miller
*Definition of the Soul,* John Skoyles
*Dithyrambs,* Richard Katrovas
*Postal Routes,* Elizabeth Kirschner
*The Blue Salvages,* Wayne Dodd
*The Joy Addict,* James Harms
*Clemency,* Colette Inez
*Scattering the Ashes,* Jeff Friedman
*Sacred Conversations,* Peter Cooley
*Life Among the Trolls,* Maura Stanton